Introduction by W. Terrence Gordon

If the creation of Planet Hollywood can be read into McLuhan's opening paragraph below, it is with an ironic twist that would have pleased him. Those who grasped McLuhan only tenuously or needed to scrutinize his pronouncements for words that could be sensationalized in the media would miss that irony as well as the irony of *sensationalism*, given that the program of media ecology advanced by McLuhan for decades revolved around developing awareness of and balance in the sensory life of mankind in the electric age. Predicting the future was not a high priority for McLuhan, and one wonders if it was in a throw-away gesture of exasperated reaction to media lackeys badgering him for predictions that he declared that stock markets would vanish by 2000 and that astronauts would be travelling in edible spaceships. Laughing at himself may have been the only out in those circumstances; what is certain is that he spoke of the necessity for humans to learn to laugh at the pomposity of moonshots. The reason emerges at the outset of this essay: "[T]he poet remains the only person able to cope with the infinite, interior spaces of our psyche." In developing this observation, McLuhan outlines the evolution of human learning and communication from pre-history to our electronic age and affirms: "Science and magic have married each other. Technology and the arts meet and mingle." So much so that the conclusion of "Space, Time and Poetry" announces "a new space-time poetry." — WTG

Space, Time and Poetry

Weaver, President of the N.B.C., 'brains' that 'through exposures on television to the great men of his time, the average man will become truly contemporaneous with his age'. This is to slant an important fact. For it has always been an advantage to have direct contact with eminent men, if only because proof positive of their essential mediocrity spurs younger talent. So long as talent is remote from those of eminence, it droops in awe and paralysis. That is the story of 'provincial' cultures. And Weaver is right to note that television helps to make the entire world one city in space. He is just as excited about this as the Italian princelings were about the printing press which, they saw, made them contemporary with the whole human past. It gave them, they felt, a superhuman citizenship in the city of the mighty dead. Renaissance meglomania was thus as much a feature of the new press as ours is tied to the exhibitionism of the camera eye and the new media. And whereas the men of the Renaissance dealt with the past as if it could be recreated as in a Hollywood set, we deal with the cosmos in the same fantasy spirit: we will start real estate schemes for the planets or make a few planets for use and amusement. But the poet remains the only person able to cope with the infinite, interior spaces of our psyche.

To go no further back than Dante, it is instructive to note his management of space. Since his entire work is visual and spatial we can dip at random. The opening of Canto V of the *Inferno* goes:

> Thus I descended from the first circle down into the second, which encompasses less space, and so much greater pain, that it stings to wailing.

Here is the generally present visual image of the cone of the Inferno which makes each descending level narrower. But he is just as interested in the auditory and tactual qualities of this space that 'stings to wailing' as in the visual:

> We paced along the lonely plain, as one who returning to his lost road, and, till he reached it, seems to go in vain. When we came there where the dew is striving with the sun, being at a place where, in the cool air, slowly it is scattered.

There is no attempt to structure the visual scene beyond the point where phrases like 'the lonely plain' or 'the dew in the sun' become means of instantly evoking mental states. Perhaps

Dante employs the visual items of simple melodic phrases, using them to define states of mind as naturally as the notes in a melody do. I think we might even say that his pre-perspective space manner gives some slight priority to the acoustic power of the verbal image. He allows the space images of his words to follow the spherical contours of the acoustic image: he invests or enspheres moments of vision with images. What appears to the eye as a flat space decorated with images and symbols is immediately felt in depth as a boundless inner or mental space.

The famous mirror scene from Canto ii of the *Paradiso* may well be a foretaste of the later perspective art.

> Three mirrors thou shalt take, and set two equally remote from thee; and let the third farther removed strike on thine eyes between the other two. Turning to them, have a light set behind thy back, enkindling the three mirrors, and, back-smitten by them all, coming again to thee. Whereas in size the more distant show shall not have so great stretch, yet thou there shalt see it needs must shine as brightly as the others.

Even here it is plain that Dante is not interested in what soon was to become enclosed visual space. Shakespeare's *Sonnet* 73 begins:

> That time of year thou mayst in me behold
> When yellow leaves, or none, or few, do hang
> Upon those boughs which shake against the cold,
> Bare ruin'd choirs, where late the sweet birds sang.

Here the time of year, designated as a mental state, is visualized swiftly in three different ways in the second line and then a fourth and fifth time in the third and fourth lines. First, bare boughs as choirs for birds of the air, and then ruined abbey choirs, as former scenes of the choir-boys' efforts, provide a superimposed visual image. The rapid transition of brief visual shots creates a kaleidoscopic sense of speed and complexity which is controlled only by the solemn music of the lines. Ben Jonson's 'Drink to me only with thine eyes' slows down this visual process greatly, but the control of the spatial items is also in the music rather than any picture-like bounding of the envisioned situation. The ordering of poetic space, as in a picture, did not occur until the theory of the picturesque in painting and of optics in physics had given pause to the forward linear movement of the line.

Wordsworth was an extremely conscious, arty practitioner of the 18th century picturesque theories and techniques, as can be seen in his *Evening Walk*, *Descriptive Sketches*, and *Solitary Reaper*:

> Behold her, single in the field,
> Yon solitary Highland Lass!
> Reaping and singing by herself;
> Stop here, or gently pass!

His visual instruction or spatial definition is given three times in three lines: 'single', 'solitary', 'by herself'.

The careful use of external landscape to evoke and explore inner states persisted until Rimbaud and the symbolists made the discovery of inner space. But Edgar Poe, as Baudelaire insisted, was the means of bringing this inner space into sharp European focus.

Now the 19th century press and telegraph effected changes in society and communications which we are only beginning to catch up with conceptually. Perhaps what has happened, in the past century especially, has been the completion of the cycle of mechanization of human learning and communication. But that cycle began in pre-history. We become aware of it only at the advanced stage when writing occurs. Writing is the translation of the audible into the visible. The translation is literally, metaphor. Recorded history is thus set upon a metaphor. Before the invention of that metaphor men had been shaping not visual but acoustical space. Oral speech is the articulation of that vague, terrifying ambience by which the ears of archaic man ensphere his being. It is by the visible spacing of pitches that he structures and controls the personal and interpersonal spaces of his world. Until men learned to translate these magical vocal gestures into visual terms, they went in awe and fear of their ordinary breath, their 'winged words'. With writing the emotionally ordered acoustical space of pitch stress gradually dimmed. But even for Aristotle the obvious fact about speech is that it is a technique of arresting the hearer's mind and fixing his attention. For a culture of readers it seems strange to define speech as a series of acoustical gestures for arresting the mind. We had long ceased to speculate on this mystery until the mechanization of speech, image, and gesture brought the wheel full circle. Today, with all our technology, and because of it, we stand once more in the magical acoustical sphere of pre-literate man. Politics have become musical; music has become politics. Government has become entertainment, and vice versa. Commerce has become incantation and magical gesture. Science and magic have married each other. Technology and the arts meet and mingle.

A recent *Fortune* ad is entitled 'Three of a Kind'. We are shown three canny gents in action. The copy begins: 'No beards, no sandals, no long hair, no frantic gestures — but artists just the same. They aren't frenetic movie directors, either, but are art directors for an advertising agency, creating an ad. They know their art all right. Theirs is the toughest job in art — creating.'

It is easy to match that ad by recalling the bizarre invasion of the artist's quarters by the rich after the First War. Wyndham Lewis' analysis of that event in *The Art of Being Ruled* remains a solitary piece of reporting and diagnosis. Today it is not the idle rich but the busy rich who are hastening to acquire squatters' rights all along the art frontiers. Why? Why should the top brass of industry and bureaucracy invade the penurious domain of the solitary artists? Perhaps because technology has itself begun to approach the mystery of the creative process? Because technology has plunged us collectively into the uncharted primitive terrors of individual artistic intuition? Has technology adopted as its province the entire human psyche and the earth which it inhabits? Are there sufficient signs that technological man is prepared to manipulate, as his matter, both earth and spirit? Have the ancient boundaries between art and nature been erased?

Since the mass production of the book began in the 16th century and with the later arrival of the popular press, magazine, movie, radio and television, it has been a tendency for the media to act less as a bridge between the individual and various segments of the outer world than for them to usury the function of that outer world. The new media have blurred the boundaries of inner and outer. The omnipresence of news and views has merged man's inner and outer life. Uninhibited mechanization is totalitarian at many levels. And this fact is merely another facet of the cycle mechanization, in returning us to the state of collectivized, emotional consciousness of archaic man.

For a century it has been evident in North America that great frustration of mind and purpose has resulted from the gap between official and unofficial education. Official institutional instruction at all levels has tried to maintain the priority of traditional verbal and written culture. Unofficial culture has been mainly non-verbal and visual. Unofficially the young have responded spontaneously and enthusiastically to the new technological environment. Their sensibilities have been shaped by the new machine forms which are themselves the product of the artistic imagination in mathematics and physics. But these forms and the popular culture linked to them have no official recognition in the traditional curriculum of verbal culture. A few Europeans like LeCorbusier and Giedion have undertaken to verbalize our technology for us. A few of our artists such as Poe, Henry James, Pound, and Eliot have in reverse order undertaken to technologize the traditional verbal world of the European.

There does exist, then, a two-way bridge between the traditional and technological worlds which are at war in Western culture. But it has been officially ignored or condemned. To travel this bridge requires of the traveller an acquaintance with the language and techniques of poetry on the one hand, and of the language and techniques of painting, architecture, and the visual world on the other. Few are prepared to acquire both languages and so the war between these worlds continues, waged witlessly in classroom and market-place alike — witless because nobody stands to gain and because it would cease automatically if the combatants knew it existed. The arts provide us with observational balloons from which to observe this conflict.

It is not an accident that Poe and Dickens appeared as titans of artistic invention to such artists as Baudelaire and Dostoevsky. Why, on the other hand, does the English world regard them as mere popular entertainers? The answer is simple: both Poe and Dickens projected in their writings the verbal equivalent of the commercialized technology which surrounded them. Dickens was a newspaperman at a time when the new impressionist devices of news coverage had been adopted to feed the high-speed steam-presses of London. English industrial technology was more advanced than European poetry and painting. Moreover English poetry and painting of the 18th century were decades ahead of the European equivalents. That is, Thomson, Blake, Sterne, Wordsworth and Shelley were using techniques of landscape for the precise delineation and control of mental stages long before the Europeans. And it was Newton's *Opticks* which gave these techniques in poetry and painting such early impetus. The discovery of the exact correspondence between the structure of the inner eye and the outer world established the study and vogue of symbolic correspondence between landscape and mental states. That technical priority was enjoyed by English poetry and painting almost until the time of Rimbaud and Cézanne. But with Rimbaud and Cézanne came the re-discovery of that inner space, of which from other points of view Dante was the master.

The revolutionary switch from the outer space of Romantic poetry to the inner spaces of symbolist art meant the discovery of the simultaneity of many times and many spaces in the inner landscapes of the mind. The juxtaposition of such times and spaces provided the form of *Illuminations*, *Ulysses* and *The Waste Land*. But such juxtapositions had long been present in the *form* of the 19th century newspaper. News coverage of the globe, made possible by the instantaneity of the telegraph, abridged external space more fantastically than Picasso ever did. The juxtaposition on a single page of human interest stories from every culture of the globe reshaped the whole urban sensibility. The consciousness of industrial man was daily formed by the jostling of many lives and many cultures. His individual life was no longer framed by the experience and perspectives of a single community or a continuous memory of a single people. The artists leaped, as always, to seize the advantages of this change, and to interpret them to men's thoughts and feelings. Poe and Dickens, however, made their move not at the privileged level of the art consciousness of a capital such as Paris. They already lived in the new conditions of collective consciousness from which the sharp individual articulation of awareness had disappeared or in which it was insignificant. London assumed this character by 1780. America was, as a continent, in this state from the same period.

As technology advances, verbalization declines—verbalization, that is to say, of the esthetic or human meaning and implications of technology. It needed a great poet-painter like Wyndham Lewis to bring the English mind (some of it) to the verbal level of awareness of this century. Book culture, which was all that came to America from Europe, was an excellent matrix for technological development, but proved mainly useless in educating eye and ear to emotional literacy about technology.

It was the English poets of the 18th century who rebelled against the linear perspectives of the printed page and who explicitly attacked book culture as an unconscious block in the sensibility of their time. Coleridge pointed out that the poetry of his own day was tending towards the flat landscape of the Chinese painters. Let us keep in mind that pictographic and ideogrammic cultures appear, unlike alphabetic ones, to be able to retain the acoustic speech pitches of pre-literate man. And acoustic cultures seem to be easily and naturally at home in inner space. Related to this, somehow, is the mysterious fact that poetry, whether Anglo-Saxon or contemporary, which develops the visual image intensely, also tends strongly towards the auditory stress. Dylan Thomas is a relevant instance, and we know how effective his work becomes on radio or gramophone. So is Pound, who, for example, was attracted to translate the Anglo-Saxon poem, *The Seafarer*:

> Bitter breast-cares have I abided,
> Known on my keel many a care's hold,
> And dire sea-surge, and there I oft spent
> Narrow nightwatch nigh the ship's head
> While she tossed close to cliffs.

His *Cantos*, from the same point of view, are a flat landscape compounded of innumerable inner and acoustical spaces. In fact, most of the small pieces of that huge architecture are scraps of conversation which comprise 'the tale of the tribe':

And they want to know what we talked about?
'de litteres et de armis, praestantibusque ingeniis,'
Both of ancient times and our own; books, arms
And men of unusual genius ...

Even more than the *Cantos, Finnegans Wake* is the ultimate whispering gallery of the human psyche, its vast nocturnal caverns reverberating with every sigh and gesture of the human mind and tongue since the beginning of time. Joyce had only to remove the date-line from an ordinary newspaper in order to turn its contents into such a timeless whispering gallery-cum-shooting alley. But it is probably the exceptional auditory powers of Joyce and Pound that led them to acoustical manipulation of the great flat landscapes of Romantic art and the new media. To order visual images in the airy dimensions of the inner ear has been their achievement. Perhaps it is this rediscovery of inner acoustical space that led Baudelaire to make the gesture of taking the 'hypocrite lecteur' into his poem. As industrial society excluded the poet, the poet devoured the society.

Not any art doctrine, then, but such complex changes as occur in the emergence of the press as art form, lead to the union of the visual and acoustical space in a new space-time poetry.

Marshall McLuhan

Space, Time and Poetry
Marshall McLuhan - Unbound (13)

ISBN: 1-58423-051-7
Library of Congress Control Number 2005927213

Marshall McLuhan Unbound Project Editors
Eric McLuhan, W. Terrence Gordon

Published in United States in October 2005 by
Gingko Press, Inc.
5768 Paradise Drive, Suite J • Corte Madera, CA 94925
(415) 924-9615 • Fax (415) 924-9608
email: books@gingkopress.com
http://www.gingkopress.com

Design, packaging and production: Die Gestalten Verlag, Berlin
Layout and Typography: onlab, Berlin
Fonts: *Dolly* by Underware, *Bullet* by House Industries
Production: Martin Bretschneider, Vinzenz Geppert
Art direction: Robert Klanten

Made in Germany